THE RUNAWAY CLOCK

written and illustrated by:
L.M. HAYNES

Copyright © 2022 by L.M. Haynes.

ISBN-979-8-9855429-0-5 (softcover)
ISBN-979-8-9855429-2-9 (eBook)
ISBN-979-8-9855429-1-2 (hardcover)

All rights reserved. No part of this book may be reproduced or transmitted in any form or by any means, electronic or mechanical, including photocopying, recording, or by any information storage and retrieval system, without permission in writing from the copyright owner. The views expressed in this work are solely those of the author and do not necessarily reflect the views of the publisher, and the publisher hereby disclaims any responsibility for them

About the Author

Laurence M. Haynes is a licensed land surveyor whose hobbies include music, sports and illustration. His interest in and love for illustration, and wanting to influence the lives of young people in a faith-filled, positive way has lead to the creation of his book and six previously published books titled The Christmas Time Travelers 1, The Littlest Patriots, The Vanishing Doorknob, The Magical Christmas Tree, Legacies and The Christmas Time Travelers 2. The father of three adult daughters, Catherine, Christina and Bernadette, Larry is an active member of St. Edward the Confessor Parish in Syosset, New York, where he and his lovely wife Amy reside.

In loving memory of our beloved puggle Lily.
Thank you for your lessons of loyalty, companionship and unconditional love.
You are forever in our hearts.

    Whenever visitors to the Mathison home stepped into the living room, their eyes would immediately be drawn to the beautiful mantle clock sitting atop the fireplace.
    Not only was the fireplace made of beautifully carved wood, but the clock itself was a true work of art. Its perfectly timed "tick-tock" and enchanting hourly chime could be heard throughout the entire Mathison home.

    The Mathison family lived in a Victorian style home in the quaint village of Trinity. Nestled in the foothills of Vermont, the village was a picture postcard of quiet, tree-lined streets, beautifully preserved Victorian homes and a town square of shops, markets and restaurants.

    Ashley and Morgan Mathison lived in the home for a number of years and were blessed with three children: Brendan who was nine years old and twin daughters, Amy and Alison, age seven.

 The Mathison children had a wonderful home life. It was the type that every child dreams of.
 Their parents were very happy together and devoted countless hours to them and their community.
 Their lives were filled with wonderful family and friends, yet the outside world was filled with such hopelessness and despair. They would always talk amongst themselves and jokingly wish that time would stand still and they could stay children forever.
 After all, hadn't adults made such a mess of the world, so why would they want to be one of them.

    One day after school, in late Autumn, Brendan, Amy and Alison were sitting in the living room of their home playing their favorite board game when the mantle clock struck 4PM. The clock's beautiful chime reminded the children of their secret wish to stay children forever.

    After dinner, the three Mathison children finished up their homework, watched some television and readied themselves for bed.

    Before they went off to bed, Brendan called out to his sisters. "Hey, Amy and Alison. Before we go off to sleep tonight, let's all make a wish for time to stand still so that we can stay children forever."

 Amy and Alison agreed with Brendan, and the three Mathison children each made the same wish before they drifted off to sleep.
 It was now a few minutes before 1AM, and all was well in the Mathison house. Brendan, Amy and Alison were all sound asleep, and the house was perfectly quiet and still.
 As the mantle clock struck 1AM, something wondrous began to happen. Instead of time standing still, as the children had wished, the hands on the face of the beautiful clock began to speed up.

 Faster and faster they went. For the next five hours, the hands of the runaway clock spun out of control.
 Then suddenly, at 6AM, almost as quickly as they began, the hands of the clock slowed and the perfectly timed "tick-tock" of the beautiful clock resumed.

 When Brendan, Amy and Alison woke up the following morning, nothing seemed the same. Their bedrooms were decorated differently, the entire house itself was furnished differently and instead of being a part of what was happening around them, they seemed to be outside observers to what was happening.

 As they slowly walked down the stairs and into the living room, they heard the sound of voices coming from the kitchen. As they peeked around the doorway leading into the kitchen, they could see five people gathered around the table enjoying breakfast.

 They recognized two of the people as their mom and dad, however they looked a bit different and a bit older. Then, to their complete surprise, they recognized the other three people at the table as themselves.

 As Brendan glanced over at a calendar hanging from a bulletin board on the kitchen wall, he realized that ten years had passed while he and his sisters slept.

 Was this a dream? Was it a nightmare? Had the wish that they made at bedtime the night before somehow come true in a very strange way?

    When Brendan, Amy and Alison realized that they could not be seen nor heard by anyone, they decided to explore this strange world they had stumbled into.
    As they huddled together in the living room, Brendan whispered to Amy and Alison, "Let's see what our world looks like in the future. I know we wished for time to stand still and for the three of us to stay children forever, but somehow the crazy wish that we made has come true in a very strange way, so let's follow where it takes us."

 Amy and Alison agreed and soon the three Mathison children stepped through the front door of their home and onto the still familiar streets of Trinity.
 As they walked through the town, Brendan could see himself as a nineteen year old, and Amy and Alison could see themselves as seventeen year olds.
 Brendan saw himself as a college sophomore at a local college. He was very happy, surrounded by many loving friends and chasing his dream of being an art major.
 Amy and Alison could see themselves preparing for their senior prom, their graduation and the college careers that awaited them in the fall.
 They all smiled when they saw themselves as teenagers.

As the day was drawing to a close, Brendan, Amy and Alison decided to return to their family home. Since they could not be seen nor heard, they entered through the front door and settled in on the living room sofa for the night.

They became very frightened that they might never return to the life they knew as children, so it took them quite awhile to fall asleep. "Please try to close your eyes and fall asleep?" Brendan asked his two sisters. "Maybe when we wake up tomorrow, we will be in our own beds, and this strange dream will be over." "We will try Brendan," Amy replied. "We will try."

    It was almost 1 AM when the three Mathison children fell asleep. When 6 AM arrived the following morning, the mantle clock chimed loudly. Brendan, Amy and Alison woke, not to find themselves in their own beds, but to find themselves still on the living room sofa.

    They walked over to the doorway of the kitchen, and this time they saw only their mom and dad sitting at the table.

    "Hey Brendan and Amy, where are we?" a troubled Alison asked. "Yesterday we were sitting at the table with mom and dad, and today we are not there."

    Brendan decided to look over to the calendar on the bulletin board, and to his amazement, found that another ten years passed.

"Well Alison, I think another ten years passed while we slept," Brendan replied. It seemed that with each passing day that they spent under the spell of their bedtime wish, Brendan, Amy and Alison could see themselves another ten Autumns into the future.

So, they once again left the safety of their home to walk the familiar streets of Trinity.

Only this time, twenty years had passed since the night of their bedtime wish. Some of the houses and buildings were changed, some were completely gone, but most were still the same.

As they walked along, they could now see themselves, their family and friends twenty years older.

 Brendan, now twenty-nine, had settled in the village of Trinity after college. His dream of being an artist came true. He saw himself married to his college sweetheart, and they had two beautiful young children.

 In their spare time, they devoted many hours to their church and to a number of soup kitchens in Trinity and in neighboring towns.

 Amy and Alison had also settled in Trinity after college. Both still single and now nurses, they worked at a children's hospital just outside of Trinity, providing care for sick children.

 Seeing the difference that they could make in the world as adults, all three began to believe that the bedtime wish that they made was a big mistake.

    As the end of the second day neared, Brendan, Amy and Alison returned to their home and settled onto the living room sofa. They were still under the spell of their strange dream, not knowing when it might end.

    As 6 AM arrived the next morning, Brendan, Amy and Alison hurried to the entrance to the kitchen. There, sitting at the table was their mom and dad and five young children. As Brendan suspected, the calendar had jumped ahead another ten years.

Although their previous two journeys from the family home showed a very positive future, Brendan, Amy and Alison were now very frightened to leave their home. They knew they would be seeing themselves thirty years into the future. What would this third day show them? What changes would come to them, their family and friends and their beautiful village?

As they left the safety of their home, they were so very happy to see that even though some sadness came into their lives and the lives of family and friends, life was still to be cherished and celebrated.

All three of the Mathison children were married and had beautiful families. They all loved the work that they were doing every day and loved even more the work that they were doing to help friends and strangers in their community. The work that they were doing as adults was making a difference.

The lessons of hope, compassion and child-like faith that they had learned from their parents were now being passed on to their children. With a child-like faith in God, the future is always full of hope and promise.

    Brendan, Amy and Alison had seen themselves thirty years into the future. They realized that their wish for time to stand still and for them to remain children forever was not very real and was not what God intended for any of them.

    As they returned to their family home, instead of sleeping on the living room sofa, they climbed the stairs and gently lay down in their beds. Brendan hurried up the stairs ahead of Amy and Alison, but they were right behind him. Even though they still could not be seen nor heard, they were quiet as church mice.

    Maybe tonight would be the night that they would return to their childhood.

    The Mathison children each prayed that the spell of their bedtime wish would be broken as they slept.

    It was once again nearing 1AM. As the mantle clock again struck 1, the hands of the clock began to spin out of control. Only this time, they were spinning backwards. For the next five hours, as Brendan, Amy and Alison slept, the hands of the runaway clock spun feverishly out of control.

    At 6AM, just as they had done 3 days earlier, the hands of the clock slowed, and the "tick-tock" of the beautiful clock once again filled the house.

    As Brendan, Amy and Alison were awakened by the six beautiful chimes of the mantle clock, they each jumped from their beds and ran into the upstairs hallway. As they looked around, they noticed that their bedrooms were decorated just as they always had been, the house was furnished exactly as it always had been and once again they seemed part of their world instead of unseen and unheard outside observers.

    As they rushed downstairs, they could hear the voices of their mom and dad coming from the kitchen. Before entering, Brendan took a long look at the bulletin board calendar.

    To his great joy, it once again had the correct date and year.

    They all gave out a loud cheer as they ran into the kitchen.

Brendan, Amy and Alison ran into the kitchen to the waiting arms of their mom and dad.

Ashley and Morgan were overjoyed by the loving embrace of their children.

"What's this all about?" Morgan asked the children.

"Nothing really, daddy," Brendan answered. "We're just very glad to see you and mom. For some reason, this morning it seems as if years have passed since we last saw you."

Actually, they had been asleep for only one night. Their bedtime wish from the night before had taken them on a journey thirty years into the future.

 Brendan, Amy and Alison learned that staying a child forever is not the answer. They were blessed to see what their lives would be like in the future. They were blessed to see how their lives would touch so many other lives.

 Perhaps we were meant to grow older, to learn as we grow and then use that knowledge to make a difference in our tiny corner of the world, instead of complaining about everything.

 Remaining a child is not the answer. Acting as a childish adult is not the answer. The answer lies in living our lives with a faith in God that is child-like and unwavering. None of us knows exactly what life has in store or where the perfectly timed "tick-tock" of our own mantle clocks will lead us, but if we live our lives believing in and loving God and trying our very best to love one another unconditionally, our path to Jesus will be assured.

    At the time the disciples came to Jesus and asked, "Who, then, is the greatest in the kingdom of heaven?"

    He called a little child to him, and placed the child among them. And he said: "Truly I tell you, unless you change and become like little children, you will never enter the kingdom of heaven."

(Matthew 18: 1-3 NIV)

www.ingramcontent.com/pod-product-compliance
Lightning Source LLC
LaVergne TN
LVHW070434070526
838199LV00014B/502